A Cabin a Pond

And Other Short Stories

By April McMurtrey with Chantel McCabe
Edited by Megan Hambly

*For use with lessons 11-20
in the Learn Reading program*

Copyright 2019 by April McMurtrey
Printed in the United States of America

Learn Reading
3717 Acadia Circle
Bakersfield, CA 93311

Visit us at: LearnReading.com

All rights reserved. No portion of this publication may be reproduced by any means, including duplicating, photocopying, electronic, mechanical, recording, the World Wide Web, e-mail, or otherwise, without written permission from Learn Reading.

V.1.1.

ISBN# 9781712667873

Contents:

Lesson 11..5

Lesson 12..13

Lesson 13..21

Lesson 14..29

Lesson 15..37

Lesson 16..45

Lesson 17..53

Lesson 18..61

Lesson 19..69

Lesson 20..77

LESSON 11

The Red Mandolin

Ben sold Otis a red mandolin to test at the polo. Otis tested it. The mandolin is so rad.

"No, bro, no!" insisted Moses, a polo pro. "The din of the mandolin midst the colts is bad. The colts bolt!"

Otis is sad. Otis sold the mandolin to Ellen. Ellen is ecstatic. "The mandolin is splendid, Otis!" Ellen insists. Ellen toted the mandolin to the polo and tested it in a solo. The timid colts bolted. Moses, the polo pro, is mad!

"I told Otis 'no mandolin'!" rants Moses.

Ellen is bold, "Otis sold the mandolin. Lasso the colts, Moses!"

Coco the Colt

Coco the colt is restless. Otis sold Coco to Ellen. "Open the cabin, Ellen. Let Coco enter. Molasses and bran is for dinner!" Otis told Ellen.

Ellen lets Coco enter. Coco is cold. "Coco, rest at the lit pit," Ellen insists. Ellen lit the lantern and sits to pet Coco. Soren, a nomad, taps the bell at the cabin. "Otis, open the cabin!" Ellen told Otis.

"I am Soren, the nomad," Soren told Otis. "I am cold and sober. I bless you for a bed to rest in."

"Enter the cabin," Ellen insists.

"A colt in a cabin? Splendid!" Soren is ecstatic. Soren sat at the pit to pet Coco and rest. Soren slept.

Stolen Coco

"Coco is stolen!" Ellen rants in a temper.

"Coco? Stolen?" Otis is mad. No Coco and no Soren in the cabin! The cabin is open. Ellen is sad.

"No, no!" Soren insists.

"Soren, enter the cabin!" Otis insists.

Soren admits, "I sent Coco to the polo for molasses and bran. I told Moses that Otis sold Coco to Ellen; Ellen and Otis slept; Coco is cold in the cabin; the molasses is limited; and the bran in the cabin is old midst mold!"

"Mold in the bran? The bran is old?" Ellen snaps.

Soren is sad. "I omitted to tell you that Coco is at the polo," Soren admits. Ellen, Otis, and Soren collect Coco.

Soren and the Rabbit

Soren, the nomad, tramps to the desert. Soren toted a present: the red mandolin. Soren is ecstatic and tested the mandolin in the desert sand. The mandolin is splendid. "A nomad is no indolent man!" Soren told no man.

Soren tramps and stamps in the desert sand. Soren sets a tent in the sand. A timid desert rabbit inspects the tent. "Old Soren can scatter bran in the sand for the rabbit!" Soren told the rabbit. The rabbit inspects and nips the bran. Soren pets the rabbit. It is cold in the desert. The lantern in the tent is lit. Soren and the rabbit test the mat in the tent and slept.

Soren, the Talented Nomad

Ellen and Otis lasso Coco the colt at the polo. Moses, the polo pro, told Ellen and Otis, "Soren, the sober nomad, is an old pro. Soren can collect colts solo in the desert. Soren is no indolent nomad and is a bold, talented man. Soren can impress!"

Ellen, Otis, and Coco tramp to the cabin. A tempest pelts the land. The cabin is cold. Ellen lit the lantern and the pit. Dinner is bland. Ellen and Otis miss Soren and tell Coco that the talented nomad is in a tent in the desert.

LESSON 12

Dinner in the Inn

Emily and Sandy enter the dimly lit inn for dinner.

"The inn is a bit smelly!" Emily insists.

"No, no, that is dinner!" Sandy admits.

Emily insists, "The inn is messy!"

"No, no, Emily! The inn is trendy and classy. It is splendid!"

Milly and Tom enter the inn for dinner. Milly is a scantily clad lass and Tom is a dressy lad. "The inn is a misery, Tom! It is nasty, smelly, messy, and clammy!" Milly insists.

"Admittedly, the inn is a bit smelly and messy," Tom admits. "It is mostly classy and trendy!"

Sadly, the dinner ends badly.

The Mandolin Act

It was cold, misty, and clammy as Avery and Sally sped to the inn. The tempest was bad. The inn was dimly lit. The entry to the inn was old. Avery and Sally enter the inn. Avery is a solo mandolin pro. Sally is bold and sold Avery's mandolin act to the inn man. "Avery is splendid and trendy! Avery is the best!" Sally insisted. The inn man let Avery test her mandolin act at the inn.

"It is a classy act, Avery and her mandolin!" the inn man admitted to Sally. Sally is so merry. Avery is mostly sober. They sit for dinner. The inn man sent a present of candy.

Mad Milly

"The nasty mandolin act is a din!" the scantily clad Milly insisted. "It is endlessly, distractedly bad!"

Dressy Tom was testy. "The mandolin act is splendid and Avery is classy!"

"Avery? Classy?" Milly was mad and spat, "I am classy! Avery can't be classy. Avery is messy, bad, and sad!"

Tom was sad. Milly was silly. The inn man sold Tom trendy candy as a present for Milly. Milly bit the candy open. Milly was still mad. Milly rented a sled and sped madly to her cabin past the tannery. "Admittedly," Tom told the inn man, "Milly is a testy, pesty misery!"

Sad Tom

Tom is sad. Milly is at her cabin. Tom sits and stabs at his dinner. "Tom!" insists the inn man, "Sit at the lit pit by Avery and Sally for dinner. Avery is splendid and Sally is merry!"

"No, no," insists Tom. "Milly is mad!"

"Milly bolted in a temper! Milly is silly." the inn man told Tom.

Tom sits at the lit pit for dinner. "Avery, the solo mandolin act is splendid. You are a pro!" Tom admits. Avery sits inertly.

Sally insists endlessly, "Avery is a master! Avery is the best!'

Milly enters the inn and blasts Tom, Avery, and Sally, "Tom is strictly a sad, bad, smelly lad!" Milly sped to her cabin on a sled.

A Mandolin for Lily

Randy and Lily inspect the mandolin. Lily tenderly tests the mandolin. It is splendid. Randy is bold, "Can the mandolin be sold to Lily?"

"Sadly, the mandolin can't be sold," Sally admits. "Avery rents the mandolin for her solo at the inn."

"It is rented? Can Lily rent a mandolin?" Randy snaps.

"Soren, the nomad, can rent a mandolin. Soren is a pal and encamps in the desert," Sally told them.

Randy is ecstatic. "Can Soren rent her a pastel mandolin?"

"No, a red mandolin," admits Sally. Lily restlessly insists they tramp to the desert on a trip to Soren so they can rent a mandolin.

LESSON 13

Enid and the Lantern

Enid taps the lit lantern and it emits an electric deterrent. "Nasty lantern!" Enid insists.

"The lantern is an electric deterrent for insects, Enid. You can't tap it. Desist!" Eden told Enid.

"I detest the lantern, Eden! It emitted a bad nip! Resell it!" Enid demands.

"Enid, that is silly and demented!" Eden insists and is stern. "Respect that the lantern emits an electric deterrent and desist."

"You can't repress me, Eden!" Enid elects to tap the lantern in a temper.

"That sentiment is to Enid's detriment!" Eden insists. Eden relents and insists that this spat is mad and bad.

The Lantern Slips

Enid pretended to sand the indented lantern tenderly. Enid detested the electric lantern. Enid elected to open the lantern and splinter the bits. It is a bad plan. The lantern emitted an electric deterrent and Enid detected it. "Demented lantern!" Enid ranted.

The lantern slips. Bits of lantern scatter. "This is bad!" Enid admitted. Eden enters the cabin. "I sanded the lantern. It slips to the mat and bits scatter!" Enid repented.

"Mend the lantern!" Eden demanded and Enid pretended to mend it.

"The electric deterrent is electricity dependent. The plastic deterrent is a splinter. The lantern is scrap!" Enid insisted. Eden is sad.

The Splendid Decanter

The presenter presented a splendid decanter to Matt. It was a present for polo. It was classy and trendy. Matt was ecstatic. "I rode Coco. The score was splendid!" Matt told Eden. Eden respected Matt's talent. Enid resented Matt's talent. Demented Enid restlessly and endlessly demanded Matt's decanter.

"No, Enid, no! I am the polo pro! The presenter presented the decanter to me!" Matt insists and reclasps the decanter.

"Enid! No!" Eden demanded. "The decanter is Matt's!" Eden predicted that Enid can't desist. The decanter was stolen and Enid intended to resell it. Eden and Matt are sad and are mad at Enid.

The Decanter Mess

"Pass Matt's stolen decanter!" Eden insists. Eden is testy and demands respect. Enid pretended to pass the splendid decanter to Eden. "Enid! That is silly and demented! I insist, pass the decanter to me!" Eden demands.

Inept Enid elected to desist. Enid reclasps the decanter and trips. Sadly, the decanter slips, snaps badly, and spills. Bits of the decanter splinter and scatter endlessly. The mat is damp. It is a mess. Eden is mad and demands, "I detest and resent a mess! Repent!" Enid repents distractedly and intermittently pretended to mend the mess tenderly. The decanter is in the bin.

No Polo for Enid

Matt told the presenter that the decanter was stolen. The presenter was sad. "Enid is bad!" the presenter insisted.

"Enid can't relent and desist. Enid is demented," Matt told the presenter. "The decanter is a mess and is in the bin."

"Ban Enid at the polo!" the presenter insisted.

Enid resented the presenter and ranted, "No Enid at the polo? Bad, mad presenter. The presenter can't ban Enid!"

Eden insisted, "No polo for Enid! You stole Matt's decanter!"

"Matt can collect the decanter. It is in the bin!" Enid told Eden.

"Enid, no! That is demented! The decanter is scrap!"

LESSON 14

The Old Roman Map

Adam was at the transatlantic terminal. Adam demanded an atlas from Brendan at the store. "In an instant!" Adam insisted. Brendan sold Adam the last atlas and an old Roman Map. "The map is splendid! Is it patented?" Adam snaps.

"No, and it is my last," Brendan told Adam.

Milt, a political radical, pets the map. "Resell it to me, Adam!" Milt demanded.

"No!" Adam insisted. "The map is critical to a trip to a distal land!

"That is dismal!" Milt spat. "A map is critical to a trip to the Alps! I demand you resell it to me!"

"No! You are a demented political animal. No!" Adam ranted.

Milt and Milly

Adam detested demented Milt. They sat at the transatlantic terminal. Adam predicted, "Milt can't nip to the radical political rally in the Alps! No map for Milt!"

Milt was mad at Adam and can't impress Milly, the madam from the capital.

"Milt is an inept man!" Milly told Adam as she sped from Milt. Milly slips and snaps her sandal. She clasps the remnant and insists, "Milt! Send me to the local medical clinic! Be practical! It is critical!"

Milt sped Milly to the distant, inland clinic in an instant. Milly limps in and demands a salad. Milly is clad in a cast at the clinic.

Milly is a Mess

Milt sat at the medical clinic. Milt is mad: no transatlantic trip, no rally in the Alps, and no picnic for radical political men in the capital! It was a total mess. Milt is sad. "Milt!" Milly ranted, "The cast entraps and cramps me! My salad is messy; my bed is messy; I am a mess!"

Milt inspects Milly. Milt told Milly, "I am a radical, political man. I can't be an instant medical man. I am practical. The picnic is at the capital!" Milt sped to the picnic at the distant capital. Milly was mad.

A Bad Lad

Milt's trip to the distant midland capital was dismal. Milt sped past the desert and the tannery. The capital was misty and clammy. The picnic for radical political men was nasty and smelly. The presenter predicted a tempest. It was dismal and Milt was sad.

Milt sped to the transatlantic terminal. Adam still sat at the terminal, the atlas and Roman Map in a plastic, padded tote. "Is Milly better?"

"No," Milt told Adam. "Milly is mostly messy and mad. Milly is in a cast and is a mess. I admit it is a scandal to cram in a transatlantic trip midst a medical matter. I am a bad lad."

The Transatlantic Trip Dinner

The transatlantic trip dinner is splendid: clam salad and red pepper. Milt and Adam rest. Milt is bold and demands, "Resell the atlas and Roman Map to me, Adam!"

"Desist, Milt!" Adam snaps. Adam plans the trip in the atlas. Milt and Adam land in the Alps. Adam rented a sled and sped to the distant inland inn. Milt is at the local terminal and is dismal. No atlas, no map! It is critical. Milt can't plan a trip to the rally.

Adam sped to the capital in the sled. The political scandal in the capital is endless. Milt rents an interpreter to plan a trip to the remnant of the radical, political rally.

LESSON 15

Mad Man Milt

Landon was a political man. He sped to Bristol to be at the rally. The random, radical masses at the rally demanded that Milt, the elected person, be respected. Landon, a dissenter, ranted endlessly, "It is demented! That dim, inept, indolent Milt is a lemon! Mad man Milt sold a ten-ton cannon to a bold nomad in the desert for a million! It is a bad mess. The second scandal was the scantily clad madam in the capital. And then he blasted a pistol at the rally!"

Adam, a local man, admitted, "Milt is bad. It is sad the masses elected that man at the ballot. He is so bad for the land. No medallion for Milt! Send Milt to prison!"

Sell the Cannon

Soren, the bold nomad, put the ten-ton cannon in the sand in the far end of the desert. The desert was distant and inland from Bristol. Soren was ecstatic as the cannon was splendid. It was a scandal that Milt sold it to Soren for a million. Can Soren resell it for a billion?

Samson told Soren it can't be sold for a billion. Samson demanded that it be sold for a million. Soren insisted, "It is to my detriment to sell the cannon. The cannon is patented and splendid. The cannon is a deterrent to the rabid men from the transatlantic land. The cannon can't be sold. The distant desert is splendid to store it." Soren blasted a melon from the cannon to test it. The bison bolted.

The Desert Men

The men in the distant desert are sad. The bison are mad. The melon blast was bad. "Soren is loco! Send the cannon to Milt, the elected man! Send it to that land! That cannon is bad for the men and bison in the desert," they insist.

The melon and cannon political scandal was endless. Milt is crimson and rants, "They can't send the cannon to this land! That cannon was sold. It is old." Milt sent a letter to the men in the desert. The men in the desert rip the letter and send the ten-ton cannon to Milt's cabin in Bristol. The cannon bends and snaps the plants at the cabin. It dents the cabin. Milt is mad at the desert men.

Milt Slips

The ten-ton cannon is at Milt's Bristol cabin. Milt is rabid. The cabin is a dismal mess. The end of the cannon snaps the plants. He inspects the cannon. Milt sits on it and slips. His pants split. Milt clasps his scalp and crimson lip. It is bad in an instant. Milt slaps the cannon and rants, "I split an atom! Send Soren to prison!"

Nelson, a respected local person, sped Milt to the medical clinic on a stallion. The clinic man inspects Milt and mimics Milt's silly antics. Milt is clad in a cast in bed and rests. Milt is a mess; no political rally for Milt!

Milly and Milt

Milly, the lass in the midst of the capital political scandal, sped to the clinic to impress Milt. Milt is still in bed in a cast. "That was a radical lesson, Milt! If you sell a ten-ton cannon for a million to a nomad you can't limit the antics and tactics from critics!" Milly insists.

Milt is mad and rants, "I plan to tramp inland to the desert men and demand they collect the cannon from my cabin!"

Milly told Milt in a sermon, "That is silly! You can't tramp in the desert and demand that! It is random! You are a bland, blimp of a man, Milt. The scandal is dismal. Rest at the clinic and mend that tendon. Dinner is scallop, salad, and lemon."

LESSON 16

Lefty the Elf

Lefty the elf fell from the lantern in the store. Lefty felt sore and limps. "Lefty, you riffraff!" scolded Fran. "No antics in the store!"

"A nasty, smelly troll was in the store!" Lefty insisted in a lisp. "The troll lifted the tin till and stole a million! The troll ran. I was mad. I misstep and slip off the lantern. I felt daft. The troll is riffraff! Nab the troll! Cast a spell, Fran!"

"The till is stolen. It can't be a million!" Fran told Lefty.

"That is no matter! That troll is still nasty riffraff!" Lefty ranted.

Fran ran after the troll. The troll ran faster. Fran cast a spell and the troll fell.

The Riffraff Troll

Fran flits in the store, lands in a spin, and clasps the till. Lefty felt the draft. "Send the troll to prison, Fran!" Lefty frets. "That is a bad, mad, demented troll!"

"I scolded the troll, Lefty! The troll felt bad and repented. The troll ran to her dad and I told her dad, Fred, the lass stole the till. The dad was mad and scolded her, too. It was a din."

Fran clasps the till. Fran is ecstatic. Lefty felt different from Fran. Lefty sniffs, "Send that riffraff troll to prison!"

After the tiff, Fran and Lefty drafted a letter to Fred to insist that the lass can't enter the store.

Enid and the Ban

After the letter, Fred was different. "My lass, Enid, is fantastic! This letter is slander. You can't ban Enid from the store!" Fred demanded in a temper.

"Enid can't enter the store, Fred. It is rebellion! The sentinel can send her to prison. It is a fact," Lefty insisted.

"Lefty, I can fill the till with a million! Enid was demented and repented. Enid can fritter the million at the store."

Fran is practical. It is a fiscal matter. A million in the till is fantastic. Fran lifted the ban and Enid can enter the store. Enid collected a stiff, felt fan; a fat, red cat; a flat flint; a daft, plastic raft; dressy denim; satin linen; a scanty frill; lemon candy; a clam salad; and a melon fritter from the store. Lefty is ecstatic!

A Troll Store

"The ton from the store can't fit in the troll cabin. It is a scandal!" Fred frets.

Enid insists, "I can open a store! A troll store!"

Fred felt daft. To fill the store till with a million was a silly plan. The aftereffect was bad. Fred is frantic. "I can rent a store for Enid! A splendid store with staff!" Fred rants.

"Rent a store at the transatlantic terminal, Fred. The total rent bill is fantastic," Lefty told Fred.

"A troll store at the transatlantic terminal? Troll riffraff can't be at the terminal, Lefty," Fred told Lefty sadly.

Fred rents a trendy store at the polo for Enid.

A Trendy Store

The trendy store at the polo is splendid. "Can you fit the stiff, felt fan; the fat, red cat; the flat flint; the daft, plastic raft; the dressy denim; the satin linen; the scanty frill; the lemon candy; the clam salad; and the melon fritter in the store, Enid?" Fred frets.

"I can fit in more," Enid insists. "The troll store is fantastic!"

The troll store is open at the polo. The polo staff enter the store. "A daft troll store for riffraff and polo staff!" the polo staff trill.

Enid sold the old, daft, random remnants for a million. Fred felt fantastic!

LESSON 17

A Cabin at the Pond

Rob and Todd rented a cabin at the pond. "Plan the trip on a map, Rob!" Todd told Rob. They sped off to the cabin in a bobsled.

"Rob, you silly clot! You are lost. The cabin is not at the pond!" Todd ranted. Todd was mad.

"I am not a silly clot!" Rob insisted. "The cabin is at the inlet!"

Rob and Todd sped in the bobsled. The cabin was at the inlet. Rob and Todd enter the cabin. "The cabin is splendid!" Rob told Todd.

Todd insisted, "The cabin is not splendid. It is bland." Todd was a snob.

"The cabin is spotless!" Rob told Todd. Todd admitted that the cabin was spotless.

The Dinner Tiff

Rob is fond of the cabin. A falcon sits on the sill.

"Put dinner in the pot!" Todd snaps. Rob put dinner in the pot: a scallion, a clam, a lemon, and plants. "Dinner is odd, Rob!" Todd insists.

Rob is cross. Rob rants, "Dinner cost a lot, Todd. It is splendid!"

"Dinner is not splendid, Rob. It is slop and a blob!" Todd insists. "Pass the melon and salad," snaps Todd.

After the tiff, Rob lit the lantern and sped off to bed. Rob is sad that Todd is a nasty lad. Todd is mad that Rob put a stop to the dinner.

The Otter

Rob and Todd trot to the inlet to spot the otter. "An otter can bob in an inlet," Todd told Rob.

"An otter can have a lot of cod for dinner," Rob told Todd.

At the inlet, Rob told Todd, "That is odd. I can't spot an otter in the inlet!"

"I can spot a distant blob! It is an otter!" Todd insisted. The blob was an otter. Rob was ecstatic.

"Cross the inlet to the otter, Rob. Offer the otter a lot of the best cod!" Todd insisted.

"I have no cod," Rob told Todd. "Let the otter be!"

A Bed for Sam

Scott put a bonnet on Sam and they sped to the cabin at the inlet on a sled.

Rob was ecstatic and told Scott, "Enter!"

"Rob, can I have a bassinet for Sam?"

"A bassinet is in the attic at the inn. I can collect it for you," Rob told Scott.

"Fantastic!" Scott was ecstatic.

Rob collected the bassinet for Sam. Sam can't fit in the bassinet. "A cot is in the attic at the inn. I can collect it," Rob told Scott. Rob collected the cot and a padded mattress from the inn. Scott put Sam in the cot and Sam slept.

Todd and Sam

"Is that a brat?" Todd spat.

Rob was cross and insisted, "Todd, that is Sam. Sam is not a brat! Sam is a splendid, tender lad!"

Sam sat on the mat and spat melon at Todd.

"Rob! Sam is ill and spat on the spotless mat. It is a mess. Collect a mop from the inn! Put a bonnet on Sam and send the lad to the clinic!" Todd demanded.

"Sam is not ill!" Scott insisted. "Sam is a messy and mostly merry lad."

"Sam is an odd, messy, smelly brat!" Todd insisted.

Sam sniffs. Rob detected a sob. Rob blasted Todd, "Stop! You can't be nasty to a tender lad!

LESSON 18

An Otter Pup

Rob, Todd, Scott, and Sam sped in a sled to the inlet. Rob spotted the otter in the inlet. A plump otter pup sat by the otter on the sand. Rob was ecstatic. "I spotted an otter pup!"

Todd plans to plunder the cod in the inlet to sell to the men in the inn. Scott told Todd, "It is a blunder to plunder the cod. Let the cod be. Cod is dinner for the otter! Let the men in the inn have salad."

Todd was upset and ranted, "The trip to the inlet is dull!"

"Cut up the plum for Sam!" Scott told the sullen Todd. Todd cut up the plum as told.

Sam has a Plum

Sam sat on a mat on the sand and spat the plum in a lump on the mat. Todd scolded Sam, "That is silly! Your mat is crimson and messy! Scott, Sam is a dud. Riffraff Sam spits and drips the plum. The mat is a nasty mess!"

"Todd! You can't insult Sam and Scott. Sam is not a riffraff dud! Sam is a pup and a pup is messy!" Rob scolded.

"Sam is not a pup! Sam is a messy lad! Sam is crimson! Sam has mumps!" Tod insisted.

"Todd, it is not mumps! It is plum!" Scott insisted.

Sam and the Pond

Rob, Todd, Scott, and Sam sped in a sled to the cabin. "Put Sam and the messy mat in the pond!" Todd demanded. "Sam has crimson scum on the scalp!"

Scott inspected Sam. Sam was a messy, smelly, crimson lad. The mat was nasty. Rob, Todd, Scott, and Sam sped to the pond. "Suspend Sam in the pond, Scott. It must be sudden! Pretend Sam is a puppet with a mullet!" Todd told Scott. Scott tenderly suspended Sam in the pond. Sam was upset. In a blunder, Scott slipped off a clod and landed in the pond. Sam was merry. Todd inspected the crimson pond scum in the sun.

Salad and Melon

They sped to the cabin. Scott and Sam were scantily clad and damp. Rob lit the lantern and put a bonnet on Sam. "Is dinner in the pot, Rob?" Todd spat.

"No, I have no dinner in the pot. I can muster salad and lemon on melon," Rob told Todd.

Todd was upset. "That is dull. I suspect the dinner at the inn is splendid. I can run to the inn for dinner!" Todd ranted.

"That is an insult. Run to the inn, Todd! Scott, Sam, and I can have salad and melon." Rob insisted. Todd ran to the inn. Sam spat a remnant of melon on the mat.

Dinner at the Inn

The dinner at the inn was fantastic and Todd was ecstatic. "No blob and slop, no crimson plum scum, no melon and salad!" Todd told the men at the inn. "A plump cut of cod on a bed of scallion and red pepper on a spotless linen mat is a splendid dinner!"

Todd sat under the upper dinner spot by the band. Amber, the mandolin pro, was splendid. The trumpet solo was fantastic. Todd sips from a cup. Todd felt a suspect cramp. It was sudden. Todd rented a bed at the inn. He can't limp to the cabin.

LESSON 19

The Velvet Set

Silver and Satin is a store on the upper story of the vessel The Boston Rebellion. Val Silver said, "Vic, a velvet vest and pants set is an investment. It is splendid for dinner, it is splendid for polo, and it is fantastic for travel! Put it on." Vic tested the velvet set and put it on. It fits. Vic felt fantastic. "Vic, tell Melvin the velvet set is an investment. They only cost a sliver!" Val insisted.

"Can Melvin test the set, Val?" said Vic.

"Melvin can inspect it!" Val said.

Melvin inspected the set and said, "It is a fantastic investment, Vic!"

The Celtic Festival

The Celtic Festival event was on the vast upper v of The Boston Rebellion. Vic put on her dressy velvet vest and pants set for the festival dinner. "Dinner at the festival is a splendid plan, Vic!" Melvin said. "Put my map in your canvas tote," Melvin said to Vic.

Dinner was the best ever: scallion, red pepper, and a plump spud.

"Fill my cup at the vat, Melvin!" said Vic.

"The festival is fantastic, Vic! I am a fan," Melvin admitted.

"Have fun, Melvin! Fill a cup at the vat!"

"No, they will evict me if I am silly!" Melvin insisted.

Vic Spills

"Pass the map, Vic." Melvin said. "The vessel sets off at ten on the transatlantic trip!"

"Invert the map and plan the trip. The Atlantic is vast," Vic said.

Melvin inspected the map and said, "The vessel will travel up the inlet and then cross the Atlantic."

A sudden blast from the vessel upset Vic and Melvin. Vic spills her cup on her velvet pants.

Vic insists, "I must visit the cabin and put on denim pants. The velvet is a mess."

"Dab your pants." Melvin passes Vic a mat. "Your pants can't be that bad. Let me fill your cup. Fun at the festival!

Vic is Ill

Val and Bob Silver from Silver and Satin met Vic and Melvin at the festival on the upper story. "Vic," said Bob, "The velvet pants set is splendid!"

"The pants are damp and I am upset," Vic said.

It is ten and the vessel sets off from the inlet. The masses on the upper story are ecstatic and clap. Then a tempest on the Atlantic blasts The Boston Rebellion. "The vessel can't be even in a bob and a dip in a tempest. I am ill!" frets Vic.

"It is the cups from the vat that have that effect, Vic!" Melvin insists. "It is not the vessel."

"I must limp to the cabin and rest," Vic said.

The Cabin

"The cabin is not the best, Melvin. It is a dud." Vic said. "It is dim and smelly. The mattress has a lump and a clump. The bed is slender. I can't fit!"

"You can't be a snob, Vic! The mattress is velvet. The bed is silver. The cabin is vast!"

"Tell the master of the vessel that the cabin is a dismal mess. It is even bad for a rat! Only the best cabin on the upper story for me, Melvin!" Vic demanded.

"That is daft! The master will put you on a raft!" Melvin said as he stamps off to the master.

LESSON 20

Matt and Melvin

Melvin stamps off to tell the master of the vessel that the cabin is dismal. Matt, an adept man, spotted sad Melvin at the festival. "There, there. What is amiss? Can I fill your cup at the vat?" Matt said to Melvin.

"I am in misery! I want to split from Vic. Vic is demented and demanded a better cabin," lamented Melvin.

"No, no," said Matt. "It is a dismal scandal! You can't split from Vic! That is abrupt and Vic will rip the cabin asunder. Vic felt ill and sad. I predict Vic is better. I have a splendid cabin on the upper story. You can put Vic there. I can have your cabin!"

Melvin is ecstatic and ran to Vic. "Tada! I have a fantastic cabin!"

Vic and the Salon

"Melvin, you are the best man! There is a plasma and an antenna. The American Arena is on! I am a fan! There is a banana, a lemon, a melon, and vanilla candy in a vessel! I can spot the Atlantic from the bed. The Boston Rebellion is splendid!" said Vic.

Melvin sent Vic to Stella at the salon for a sun lamp bed stint and to Bella for a crimson tint. Vic felt fantastic!

Brenda from Tacoma was at the salon. Brenda was a cadet and had the ability to be abrupt. "A cut and tint!" said the sullen Brenda to Bella. Bella sent Brenda to the festival to distract her till Vic was splendid.

Ten Million from Banana

Brenda met Matt at the festival. "I am a talented cadet from Tacoma. Delta sent me here on this trip," said Brenda.

"A Delta cadet? You impress!" said Matt. "I am a man from Africa. I had the ability to amass ten million from banana!"

"Ten million from banana? That is a fantastic statistic!" Brenda said.

"Big banana is a fantastic fiscal matter, Brenda. To resell banana is the best!" Matt admitted.

"I bet!" Brenda said. Matt was different from Santa. Matt was better!

"I am on this transatlantic trip to Africa, Brenda. My trip to the Banana Summit in Boston is past and my American banana patent matter is ended," Matt said. Brenda was upset.

"Can we have dinner at the festival?" said Matt.

The Festival Dinner

Brenda and Matt sit at the festival arena for dinner. "You are an adept cadet!" Matt said.

"There is cod and spud for dinner," said Alma, a festival lass, to Brenda and Matt.

"No salmonella cod for me!" Brenda said. "A salad and a banana fritter is fantastic!"

"There is no salmonella on the vessel!" insists Alma.

Matt selects scallion, spud, and a banana fritter.

"Is that Melvin and Vic, there at the vat? A tan and a crimson tint for Vic?" said Matt. "Melvin and Vic! Sit for dinner!" Matt insists.

"Matt presented the ability to amass ten million!" Brenda told Vic.

Matt and Brenda

The Boston Rebellion sped from America to Africa. They enter the African capital. Upset Brenda lamented and said, "Send a letter, Matt!" Matt clasps Brenda and presents vanilla and banana candy to her.

"Brenda, you are splendid. You are an adept cadet. I respect you. After Delta, travel to Africa and be banana staff for me!" Matt said and left the vessel.

The vessel left Africa. Melvin and Vic adopted the sad Brenda. Vic said, "Matt is a one in a million man, Brenda!"

"I am a banana man statistic!" Brenda sniffs. Brenda sat at the vat and Melvin filled her cup.

Great Job!

*You are ready for the next book,
<u>The Banana Summit Dinner Dance</u>!*

Like this book?

To order additional stories
intended for use with the Learn Reading
program, or to order the full
LEARN READING PROGRAM
Please visit: *LearnReading.com*

Learn Reading is a "real-world" reading acquisition program designed for learners of all ages. It introduces letters and sounds one at a time in the order they appear in everyday English print. Learn Reading also provides comprehensive instruction and opportunity for development in each of the following areas:

- Phonemic awareness
- Decoding
- Sight words
- Vocabulary
- Fluency
- Accuracy and control
- Controlled blending
- Comprehension

Learn Reading integrates several multisensory learning techniques to engage the student and set them up for success. It draws on their prior knowledge, encourages curiosity, and allows them to employ their individual talents to supplement their instruction!

Best of all, the instruction is in video format! The teacher comes to you!

Visit *LearnReading.com* to learn more!

Made in the USA
Monee, IL
15 February 2024